JI-NONGO-NONGO
MEANS RIDDLES

JI-NONGO-NONGO
☷MEANS RIDDLES☷

by VERNA AARDEMA   illustrated by JERRY PINKNEY

FOUR WINDS PRESS

NEW YORK

ESEA Title IV

For reprint permission, grateful acknowledgment is made to:

Adam and Charles Black for three riddles from *The Essential Kafir,* by Dudley Kidd.

Funk and Wagnalls Publishing Company, Inc., for two riddles from *Funk & Wagnalls Standard Dictionary of Folklore, Mythology, and Legend,* edited by Maria Leach, copyright, © 1949 by Funk & Wagnalls Publishing Company, Inc.

Horizon Press for a riddle from *Yes and No, The Intimate Folklore of Africa* by Alta Jablow, © 1961 by Alta Jablow.

Macmillan & Company for a riddle from *Liberian Folklore* by Doris Banks Henries.

Oxford University Press for four riddles from *The Masai, Their Language and Folklore,* by Claud Hollis, and for eleven riddles from *Hausa Folk-lore, Customs, Proverbs, Etc.,* by Robert Sutherland Rattray.

Seeley, Service & Cooper, Ltd., for four riddles from *Wild Bush Tribes of Tropical Africa,* by G. Cyril Claridge.

Library of Congress Cataloging in Publication Data

Aardema, Verna.
  Ji-nongo-nongo means riddles.

  Bibliography: p.
  Summary: Presents a collection of riddles from Africa.
  1. Riddles, African—Juvenile literature.
  [1. Riddles] I. Pinkney, Jerry. II. Title.
  PN6371.5.A25   398.6'096   78-4038
              ISBN 0-590-07474-1

Published by Four Winds Press
A division of Scholastic Magazines, Inc., New York, N.Y.
Text copyright © 1978 by Verna Aardema
Illustrations copyright © 1978 by Jerry Pinkney
Printed in the United States of America
Library of Congress Catalog Card Number: 78-4038
1 2 3 4 5   82 81 80 79 78

This is my answer to Boys and Girls

—they asked *me* riddles when I was a teacher.

By the same author

Tales from the Story Hat
Tales for the Third Ear
Behind the Back of the Mountain
Why Mosquitoes Buzz in People's Ears
Who's in Rabbit's House?

JI-NONGO-NONGO
❖ MEANS RIDDLES ❖

Congo

Who can trust his money to a monkey?
Answer: The man who can climb trees.

Congo

Who can whistle with another man's mouth?
Answer: The other man.

Yoruba

When will a man not go to bed, even though it is night?
Answer: When his house is on fire.

Yoruba

When does a man run through thorn bushes?
Answer: When something is chasing him.

Congo

What can a dog do that a man can not?
Answer: Lick his own back.

Congo

Why shouldn't you grow pumpkins on the side of a hill?
Answer: Because when they are ripe, they would roll down.

Yoruba

What does the pig do after wallowing in the mud?
Answer: He looks for a clean person to rub against.

Yoruba

What does the pin say to the kente cloth?
Answer: Don't hang your troubles on my neck!

Yoruba

What thing in the forest frightens even the lion?
Answer: The forest fire.

Yoruba

Who is the long thin trading woman who never reaches the market?

Answer: The canoe left at the landing, while its owner goes on to the market.

Accra

When is it safe to play with the leopard cubs?
Answer: When their mother is far away.

Krahn

How does one cure a bad sore?
Answer: With a bad medicine.

Yoruba

Who has a house too small for guests?
Answer: The tortoise.

Ga

What is soft and flat, but cannot be slept upon?
Answer: The surface of the lake.

Ga

What leaps down the mountain, but cannot climb back
up?
Answer: The mountain stream.

Yoruba

What can the buffalo do that two strong men can not?
Answer: Grow horns.

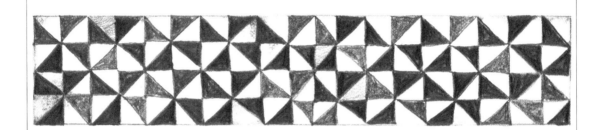

Yoruba

What is ugly when young and beautiful when full-grown?
Answer: The grub that becomes a butterfly.

Yoruba

What is long and can be shortened by the feet, but not
        with a hatchet?
Answer: The path.

Ga

What is it that you look at with one eye, but never with two?

Answer: The inside of a bottle.

Yoruba

They cut off its head. They cut off its feet. And its middle calls the town together. What is it?

Answer: A drum.

Oji

Bush-pig dies, Mangudu eats him. Kudu dies, Mangudu eats him. Mangudu dies, nobody eats him! Who is Mangudu?

Answer: The cooking pot.

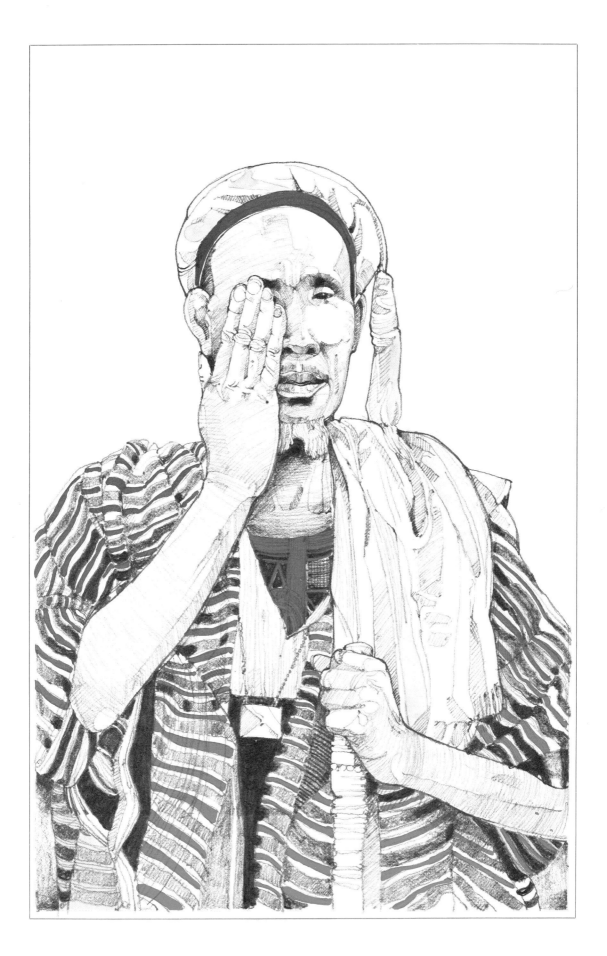

Accra

Why does a boy poke a stick into a snake hole?
Answer: Because he wouldn't dare to put his hand into it.

Hausa

What looks at the valley, but never goes into it?
Answer: The hill.

Wolof

What is long but has no shadow?
Answer: The road.

Kanuri

What is it that even the ostrich with its long neck and
        sharp eyes cannot see?
Answer: What will happen tomorrow.

Masai

What doesn't run from the prairie fire?
Answer: The bare spot.

Masai

I have two skins—one to lie upon and the other to cover
        me. What are they?
Answer: The ground and the sky.

Wolof

When does the mouse say, "Nye, nye, nye!" to the cat?
Answer: When her hole is near.

Kafir

Who is the quiet little boy who is dressed at night and left
bare in the daytime?
Answer: The clothes peg.

Kafir

What is the longest snake in the world?
Answer: The road.

Wolof

What kind of tree cannot shade you?
Answer: One that is smaller than you are.

Hausa

What can make the woodcutter throw down his ax?
Answer: The little biting ants that fall from the tree.

Hausa

What lies down when it's hungry and stands up when
it's full?
Answer: A rice sack.

Masai

What does a cow say when it is about to be sold?
Answer: "Strike a hard bargain! For the man who pays a
    long price will treat me well."

Hausa

When do you pat the cow?
Answer: Before you milk her.

Hausa

Who doesn't get lost in the forest in the daytime?
Answer: The person who doesn't get lost there at night.

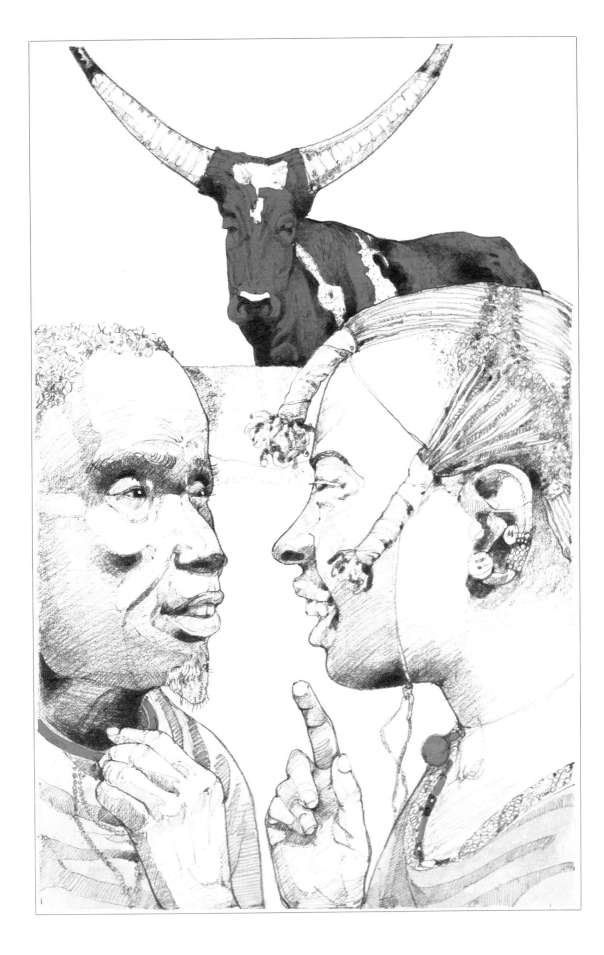

Masai

Who has more courage than a Masai warrior?
Answer: Two Masai warriors.

Hausa

Who won't listen when you tell him to stop?
Answer: The child who has never had a spanking.

Hausa

When do the mice play in the corn bin?
Answer: When the cat is not around.

Hausa

Why is a man like a pepper?
Answer: Until you have tested him, you can't tell how
strong he is.

Kafir

Who is it that always stands, and never sits down?
Answer: A tree.

Hausa

What sleeping creature should never be touched?
Answer: The scorpion, because its stinging tail never
sleeps.

Hausa

If the chief commands everyone to weep and fill a
   calabash with tears, what does the person with one
   eye do?

Answer: He weeps twice as hard.

Hausa

When does the hen fear the hawk?
Answer: When she has baby chicks.

Bibliography

Burton, Richard R. *Wit and Wisdom of West Africa.* London: Tinsley
    Brothers, 1865.

Claridge, Cyril. *Wild Bush Tribes of Tropical Africa.* London: Seeley,
    Service and Company, 1922.

Henries, Doris Banks. *Liberian Folklore.* London: Macmillan & Co., Ltd.,
    1966

Hollis, Claud. *The Masai, Their Language and Folklore.* London:
    Oxford at the Clarendon Press, 1905.

Jablow, Alta. *Yes and No, The Intimate Folklore of Africa.* New York:
    Horizon Press, 1961.

Kidd, Dudley. *The Essential Kafir.* London: Adam and Charles Black,
    1904.

Leach, Maria, ed. *Standard Dictionary of Folklore, Mythology, and
    Legend.* Vol. I. New York: Funk and Wagnalls, 1949.

Lobagola, Bata Kindai Amgoza Ibn. *Folktales of a Savage.* London:
    Alfred A. Knopf, 1930.

Rattray, Robert S. *Hausa Folk-Lore, Customs, Proverbs, Etc.* Vol. II.
    London: Oxford at the Clarendon Press, 1913.

Notes

The source for the riddles from the Accra is *Wit and Wisdom of West
Africa.*

The source for the riddles from the Congo is *Wild Bush Tribes of
Tropical Africa.*

The source for the riddles from the Ga is *Wit and Wisdom of West Africa.*

The source for the riddles from the Hausa is *Hausa Folk-Lore, Customs,
Proverbs, Etc.*

The source for the riddles from the Kafir is *The Essential Kafir.*

The source for the riddles from the Kanuri is *Wit and Wisdom of West Africa.*

The source for the riddles from the Krahn is *Liberian Folklore.*

The source for the riddles from the Masai is *The Masai, Their Language and Folklore.*

The source for the riddles from the Oji is *Wit and Wisdom of West Africa.*

The source for the riddles from the Wolof is *Wit and Wisdom of West Africa.*

The source for the riddle from the Yoruba on p. 2 is *Yes and No, The Intimate Folklore of Africa.*

The source for the riddles from the Yoruba on p. 14 is *Standard Dictionary of Folklore, Mythology, and Legend.*

The source for the riddles from the Yoruba on pp. 4, 6, 8, 10, and 12 is *Wit and Wisdom of West Africa.*

398.6   Aardema, Verna.
AAR
         Ji-nongo-nongo means
         riddles.
                              6.25

398.6   Aardema, Verna
AAR   Ji-nongo-nongo
         means riddles.

DATE DUE

JUN. 1 4 1993		
hosser		
APR. 1 5 1997		